ENGLISH SEASIDE

THE ENGLISH SEASIDE

Peter Williams

ENGLISH HERITAGE

Published by English Heritage, NMRC, Kemble Drive, Swindon SN2 2GZ
www.english-heritage.org.uk
English Heritage is the Government's statutory adviser on all
aspects of the historic environment.

10 9 8 7 6 5 4 3 2

Product code 51230
ISBN-10 1 905624 02 6
ISBN-13 978 1 905624 02 7

British Library Cataloguing in Publication Data
A CIP catalogue for this book is available from the British Library.

Edited and brought to publication by Susan Kelleher
Designed by Rod Teasdale
Printed by Bath Press

FRONT COVER: **Weymouth, Dorset**
PAGE 1: **Plaque at Bognor Regis, West Sussex**
PAGE 2: **A summer's day at Weymouth, Dorset**

Contents

Introduction 6

The natural coast 8

Fishing 10

Lighthouses 16

Time and tide 20

Weather 24

Wrecks 26

Lifeboats 28

War and peace 34

Religion 46

Bathing 52

On the beach 56

Punch and Judy 60

Donkeys 64

Piers 66

Beach huts 76

Cliff lifts 84

Hotels 86

Wooden walls 92

Caravans and chalets 96

Seaside architecture of the 1930s 98

Shelters 102

Telephone kiosks 108

Something to sit on 110

Public conveniences 116

Contemporary seaside sculpture 118

Seaside gardens 122

Model villages 128

Bandstands 130

Amusements 132

Helter-skelters 142

Carousels 146

Golf 148

Food 150

Famous people 162

Palmists and clairvoyants 166

Joke shops 168

A nice cup of tea 170

Staring out to sea 172

Index of places 175

Introduction

There is a powerful sense of place at the seaside. You know what to expect.

Fishing villages usually have a quay, boats, lobster pots, and masses of seagulls while resort towns have esplanades, piers, grand hotels and gardens. Certain seaside towns have just about everything: Weymouth, for example, has a grand parade of hotels, a wide esplanade and a small fishing village. Blackpool has *more* of everything – three piers, miles of hotels, the Tower, Winter Gardens, trams, illuminations – but no fishing and no castle!

However, the 'landscape' of the typical resort is changing. Contraction of the fishing industry has had an enormous effect, but there are subtle and continuous small losses at 'street furniture' level, of ironwork railings, street lamps, shelters and seats due to the inevitable decay found when you blow salty water at the seafront. Scenic railways and helter-skelters are fast disappearing along with the time-warp 1950s' cafes and traditional candyfloss machines. Fresh fish shops are a great rarity, flowerbeds are decreasing, signwriters have signed off and where oh where can you get 'a pot of tea for the beach'? That stalwart of the hot Bank Holiday, the 'grockle' with knotted handkerchief hat, rolled-up corduroys and sandals with black socks is gone for ever.

But the changes aren't all bad. A large amount of new stainless steel street furniture is in evidence and public sculpture has proliferated, some good, some indifferent, some strange, such as Morecambe's birds. Folkestone is planning a 2-mile sculpture walk. There is a massive regeneration of seafronts under way all round the coast: Bridlington had led the way with its emphasis

TOP LEFT The Royal Pavilion, Brighton, East Sussex. The building was completed in 1823 by John Nash for King George IV.

CENTRE LEFT Blackpool Tower, Lancashire. Opened 1894, architects Maxwell and Tuke, steel erectors Bell and Wilcox of Formby.

BOTTOM LEFT Tate St Ives, Cornwall. Opened 1993, architects Shalev and Evans.

on renewal rather than replication, and both Southport and Dover have exciting new esplanades. The Tate gallery has revitalised St Ives and the same effect is anticipated in Margate.

What, you might ask, are my qualifications for writing about the seaside? Although born in Derbyshire, my early years were spent in Northern Ireland, where I lived within walking distance of a rocky beach. When I was a teenager, we had a house backing onto sand dunes at Ainsdale, near Southport, and I would often walk or cycle along the old railway line to Pleasureland in Southport to spend many an afternoon in the 'Funhouse'. Happy days. I subsequently spent three years at Blackpool, an interesting contrast to Southport!

Growing up at the seaside has its problems when you want to go for a holiday. If you already live at a resort, why go to another one?

It was in the summer of 1992 when I first set forth on my madcap mission to photograph the coast of England. My work as an architectural photographer took me all over the country and I would often stay at the seaside because that was where there were plentiful, and cheap, hotels. Long summer evenings left me with time to explore, camera in hand. Sometimes the sun shone – but mostly I never minded about the weather. The 'survey' was never meant to be about photographs as art but simply a snapshot of the seaside at a time of great change. I also wanted to expand the National Monuments Record's photographic coverage of places that had a strong sense of place but few buildings of individual merit.

As the survey progressed I began to rationalise its scope. I realised I would never get to the more remote parts of the coast and that major ports like London, Bristol, Liverpool and Hull were too big, and the dockyards difficult of access. Gradually I came to concentrate on 'resorts' and became more willing to venture inland – but only a few streets! Some seaside towns get short shrift due to lack of time and so I apologise to places I didn't have time to visit or cover properly.

For too long the seaside has suffered from bad press reports. It is accused of being tatty, of being moribund, of being the 'Costa Geriatrica'. Cold, grey, windswept, raining, it may be at times, and inevitably it has all the shortcomings of society at large – alcoholism, gambling, drugs and the rest. But I have found the seaside to be warm-hearted, welcoming and positive. It's not simply the ozone that draws the visitor to the comfort of a hotel with sea views, but some inner need to commune with nature and return to the sea. It's also about having a bit of fun – riding the rides for a thrill and a scare, seeing the shows and playing the machines. Above all, it is to have the freedom to wander and to build castles, dam streams and bury Dad up to his neck in the sand.

The regeneration of the seaside proceeds apace – so don't you think it's time to rediscover what a fantastic place it is – full of character, charm and 'Englishness'! You'll find there's no truer words than those expressed in the old music hall song:

Oh! I do like to be beside the seaside,
I do like to be beside the sea.
I do like to stroll along the prom, prom, prom,
Where the brass bands play
Tiddley-om-pom-pom!

Oh! Just let me be beside the seaside,
I'll be beside myself with glee,
And there's lots of girls beside
I should like to be beside
Beside the seaside!

Beside the sea!

Peter Williams
June 2005

The natural coast

A surprising amount of the English coast is in its natural state, unaltered by harbours, sea-walls or works of civil engineering. Outside the major port areas and conurbations, you can walk for miles without seeing anyone.

This solitary, even lonely, aspect of the coast is its chief attraction for many. The combination of big sea and big sky is a powerful spiritual magnet, and there is also something of the desert in an endless beach. It is a place where, whilst we contemplate the infinite grains of sand or gaze out to sea, we can reflect on the meaning of life and our own inner selves. That is, if it doesn't rain.

BELOW A lone figure has a Robinson Crusoe moment as she stumbles upon a line of footprints in the sand at Filey beach, North Yorkshire.

ABOVE Atlantic breakers and pebbles at Porth Nanven, Cornwall.

The question is – just what is 'wild', 'natural' and 'unaltered' and what is carefully and discreetly 'managed'? We like the thought of a natural environment, but at the same time somehow expect the shoreline to be watched over by Coastguards, Customs and the National Trust. Some management is necessary for safety and to protect rare plants and animals – but let's not be constricted by too many rules and regulations.

Some 'wild' and 'natural' areas are subject to heavy pressure from tourists. The Valley of the Rocks near Lynton and Lynmouth attracted the attention of Gainsborough, Wordsworth, Shelley, Coleridge and Conan Doyle and is still a very real area of outstanding natural beauty. It is now a 'managed' wilderness and you have to park in designated places and keep to the paths. The 'wild' coastal sand dune areas of Upton Towans, Formby Point and Druridge Bay are popular destinations but susceptible to pathway erosion and need constant repair. Pebbly beaches can be at risk from the relentless removal of stones for souvenirs and garden makeovers – Crackington Haven is but one example.

For a real sense of remoteness you could explore the coast at Morecambe Bay, Silloth, or from Amble to Berwick-upon-Tweed. How about Spurn Head, The Wash, Dungeness and Camber, the Isle of Portland, Watchet, Start Point, Lizard Point, Hartland Point – in fact all the sticky-out points? Everyone who likes a good remote beach will have their own special place. The thing is not to tell anyone else, or everyone will want to go and the carpark builders will move in.

TOP Sea, sand and dunes near Bamburgh, Northumberland, with the Farne Islands glittering on the horizon.

MIDDLE The Pulpit Rock at Portland Bill, Dorset. Portland stone is an oolithic limestone much used as a building material.

BOTTOM The lonely sea and the sky at Caister-on-Sea, Norfolk.

Fishing

Everyone loves a fishing boat – especially if it's wooden and being freshly painted by an old tar in a blue knitted jumper. It brings out the urge to use all your old sea-fishing vocabulary – 'Avast there, me hearty'; 'Shiver me timbers!'; 'Batten down the hatches', 'Splice the mainbrace!'. Old nets, lobster pots and dive-bombing seagulls are a necessary part of every seaside resort experience. Except Blackpool and Southport!

Real fishing on an industrial scale is, of course, more to do with diesel engines and ice factories and distribution and quotas and is less attractive to the tourist.

Along with the decline in deep-sea fishing there has been the gradual disappearance of local fish shops, the transformations of fishermen's stores and net shops into holiday homes, the construction of yachting marinas and the filling of harbours with pleasure craft.

Whilst you look in vain for the Fleetwood fishing fleet, there still remains Brixham and Newlyn and the countless small harbours that still have a few boats left. If you want to look around a trawler, go to the National Fishing Heritage Centre at Grimsby and climb aboard the *Ross Tiger*.

BELOW **Polperro harbour, Cornwall.**

ABOVE Real fishing at the north landing, Flamborough, East Yorkshire.

ABOVE The visitors' carpark, Port Isaac, Cornwall.

ABOVE A sign on the side of a warehouse in Newlyn, Cornwall. Stevenson's have lovely hand-painted signs dotted about the harbour and even on the sides of their lorries.

RIGHT The Huer's Hut or House, Newquay, Cornwall. Listed as dating from the 18th century, the hut was used as a shelter for the pilchard shoal look-out. The look-out or 'huer' would call out 'Hevva hevva' and wave bushes to direct the boats. Thought to be the origin of the expression 'hue and cry'. But wait, the sign on the building says it dates from the 14th century, was originally a beacon lighthouse and then a hermitage. An interesting enigma!

ABOVE
A painting of the village displayed at the entrance to Craster, Northumberland.

RIGHT
Two rough-and-ready fish-smoking houses at Southwold, Suffolk.

PREVIOUS PAGE
TOP LEFT
The distinctive Filey cobles on the landing at this North Yorkshire seaside resort. Few now remain.

CENTRE LEFT
Boats outside the net shops at Hastings, East Sussex.

TOP RIGHT
A glimpse of the net shops at Hastings, East Sussex.

RIGHT
A small fishing boat drawn up on the beach at Worthing, West Sussex.

LEFT The town's coat-of-arms displayed on a lamp standard at Worthing, West Sussex.

TOP RIGHT Peter French Oyster Farm hut at West Mersea, Essex.

CENTRE RIGHT A fisherman's hut converted from a railway carriage at Southwold, Suffolk.

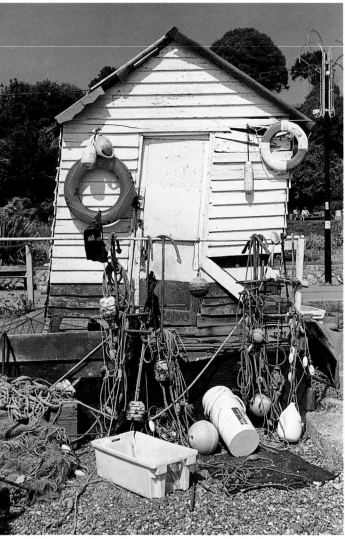

ABOVE Weatherboarded sail lofts at Brightlingsea, Essex.

LEFT The Fryer and Goodall fish shop hut at Felixstowe, Suffolk.

RIGHT A sign at Padstow, Cornwall.

LEFT A pub sign at Whitby, North Yorkshire.

RIGHT A green-tiled shopfront at Robin Hood's Bay, North Yorkshire. The large sash window is a common feature of fish shops.

BELOW Trips to the Farne Islands from Seahouses, Northumberland.

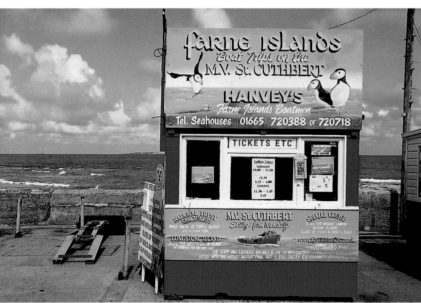

ABOVE An advertising sign for deep-sea fishing trips at Ilfracombe, Devon. Lerina is a lemon liqueur made at Chambarand Abbey in France.

RIGHT The ubiquitous fibreglass fisherman in his sou'wester. This one is at North Shields, Tyne and Wear.

LEFT Manx kippers shipped to Fleetwood, Lancashire, in order to be posted to your home. You know it makes sense.

Lighthouses

The main thing about lighthouses is that they are meant to be seen far out to sea – giant candles visible by day and night. They serve as warnings of danger and help determine position. They may be identified by the character and duration of the flash, or the paintwork on the tower which is often alternate stripes of red and white. No two are the same or else there would be total confusion. They have gradually become less important to navigation with advances in global positioning technology.

Automation has led to the loss of the Lighthouse Keeper, although someone must still be on hand to change the bulbs. I have been lucky enough to have talked to several keepers prior to automation hoping to find out what they thought about during all that gazing out to sea. Alas, they were disinclined to talk to me, being solitary types who answer all questions with the 'Maybe it will and maybe it won't' kind of reply.

LEFT **The Roman Pharos at Dover Castle, Kent, next to the church of St Mary-in-Castro. Built as a fire tower c 130 AD to guide the ships of the Classis Britannica. The top part is the remains of a medieval belfry.**

RIGHT **The unusual brick lighthouse at Gorleston-on-Sea, Norfolk, which was built in 1887.**

ABOVE The East Lighthouse at Sutton Bridge on the River Nene in Lincolnshire, formerly the home of Sir Peter Scott. In 1981 I was sent to photograph the strangely tapering built-in cupboards here and remember well the eerie mists, and weird echoing bird calls in this idyllic and remote haven.

ABOVE RIGHT The west harbour light at Newhaven, East Sussex. The light is just visible in the little oriel window on the right of the house. The whole thing is on rails and could once have been trundled back and forth.

BELOW The former Calshot Spit lightship at Southampton, Hampshire. Dating from 1914, it is now a museum. Another interesting lightship can be found at Tollesbury in Essex where Fellowship Afloat have their activity centre on board a former Trinity lightship dating from 1954.

ABOVE The 'Red Robot' at South Shields, Tyne and Wear, which was constructed in 1880.

ABOVE The lighthouse on St Mary's Island at Whitley Bay, Tyne and Wear, which was awarded 'Pointy Attraction of 2003' by the *Whitley Bay Citizen*. Built in 1898 it is now a museum.

ABOVE The only independently run operational lighthouse in Britain at Happisburgh, Norfolk.

ABOVE Smeaton's Tower, The Hoe, Plymouth, Devon. It was built on the Eddystone reef in 1759 and removed to The Hoe in the 1880s.

ABOVE A triangular sighting tree at Workington harbour, Cumbria.

ABOVE The Low Lighthouse at Burnham-on-Sea, Somerset, constructed in 1832 after the High Lighthouse proved to be built on too low a vantage point to take account of the massive rise and fall of the tides.

ABOVE The well-known lighthouse at Portland Bill, Dorset, 1906.

ABOVE On the pier at Seahouses, Northumberland. No room for a stair, so the door must open inwards to a ladder.

ABOVE The seaward side of the Beachy Head lighthouse, East Sussex, depicted on a pub sign.

ABOVE The fresnel lens on the Dungeness Old Lighthouse (1904) in Kent.

Time and tide

ABOVE **At Lyme Regis, Dorset, a sundial of 1903 harks back to more ancient times.**

The science and philosophy of time is not a subject that immediately springs to mind when strolling down the prom wearing a 'kiss me quick' hat. What are we to make of all these different meridians, Flamsteed's, Halley's, Bradley's and Airy's? What indeed do we think of the Mean Sun, an imaginary body moving round the equator with a constant speed making one circuit with respect to the vernal equinox in one tropical year? We walk on, comfortable in the knowledge that someone understands it all and we can enjoy the visible results – the many fine and interesting clock towers and clock cases built for civic pride, for jubilee, for amusement.

Accurate timekeeping is essential for navigation and it is no surprise that a great sea power was in the forefront of its development. In 1714 the Board of Longitude offered a prize of £20,000 for an accurate seagoing chronometer – finally awarding the prize in 1776 to John Harrison, a joiner from Lincolnshire. Later, the coming of the railways encouraged the standardisation of time into zones, enabling timetables to work.

LEFT **The latitude and longitude marker at Ventnor, Isle of Wight, presented by Sir Thomas Brisbane in 1851.**

RIGHT **Sheerness Dockyard, Kent. The rather 'American'-looking weatherboarded clock tower, formerly part of the Quadrangle storehouse of 1824.**

LEFT The high-tide indicator at Budleigh Salterton, Devon, in giant pocket-watch style.

BELOW The Tim Hunkin and Will Jackson water clock on Southwold pier, Suffolk.

In Brighton, however, they don't like clocks and every year, on the shortest day, hundreds of effigies of clocks are taken down to the beach and burnt.

Space precludes showing my other favourites: the water clock at Felixstowe; the station clock tower at Cleethorpes; Grange-over-Sands' clock tower; Shanklin clock tower and drinking fountain, and the unusual concoction at Herne Bay.

ABOVE The Shuttleworth clock tower at Scarborough, North Yorkshire. This features in the television series 'The Royal' centred on the fictional St Aiden's Royal Free Hospital. Arthur Shuttleworth presented the clock in 1911 as a memorial of the coronation of George V. He also later presented the gardens surrounding the clock which were originally called Red Court Gardens.

ABOVE **Deal Time Ball Tower, Kent.** Built in 1795 as a naval semaphore station to communicate with London via repeater stations, it was converted to a time ball clock in 1855. The ball was raised halfway at 12.55pm, fully raised at 12.58pm and dropped at 1pm. The ball was dismantled in 1927, but has since been replicated, and the tower is now a museum.

LEFT The high-tide indicator at Ventnor, Isle of Wight, on the gable of Blake and Sons' beach store.

RIGHT The Jubilee Clock Tower of 1887 at Weymouth, Dorset, is made of cast iron and was the gift of Sir Henry Edwards. The listed building entry describes it as, 'A florid but characteristic enrichment of the sea-front, boldly coloured.'

ABOVE LEFT The Jubilee Clock tower at Skegness, Lincolnshire, erected by public subscription in 1898 and opened by the Countess of Scarborough.

ABOVE The pillar clock at Whitley Bay, Tyne and Wear. The saving grace of a rather worse-for-wear esplanade.

LEFT The clock at the Lizard lighthouse, Cornwall, which was made by Brockbank and Atkins.

RIGHT The Jubilee Clock tower at Exmouth, Devon, architects Kerley and Ellis.

Weather

The cold, the wind, the driving rain, the leaden skies –
why do we keep going back? Well, just dive into a 'caff'
or an amusement arcade, or a winter garden, or go to
the pictures, or sit and read. All that bad weather will
soon go by and the sun will come out. And there are
spectacular sunsets. Always look on the bright side.

BELOW **Cromer Climatological
Station, Norfolk.** The
information board has been
ripped off but the rest of the
equipment appears to be well
protected against all comers.

RIGHT Not only time and tide
indicated here at Bridlington,
East Yorkshire, but also
pressure and temperature
(subject to the replacement of
the missing thermometer).

LEFT The George Hanson memorial clock and barometer at Staithes, North Yorkshire.

ABOVE Hastings Weather Kiosk, East Sussex. This is a very worthy thing. The data is gathered in White Rock Gardens and then transferred to the kiosk.

BELOW A detail of the weather kiosk instrumentation.

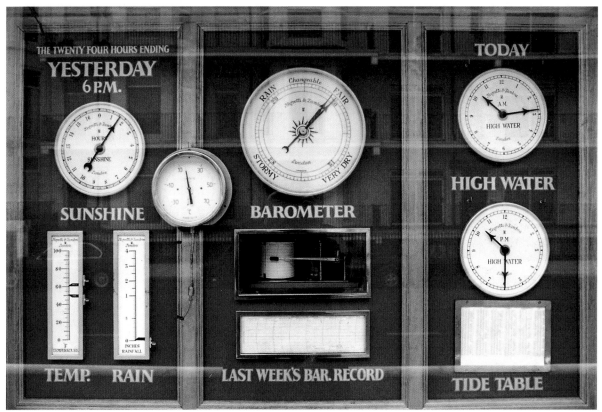

Wrecks

The coast of Britain is surrounded by countless wrecks wherever there are hazardous rocks or shallow waters. Most wrecks, of course, are underwater and invisible. Some are occasionally revealed by wind or tide and we can marvel at their wood or metal bones sticking up from the sand and hope there was no loss of life. A real must-see wreck is the Bronze Age boat at Dover Museum.

ABOVE **Fishing boats are often drawn up on the beach at Newlyn, Cornwall,** to be ignominiously broken up and even burnt.

ABOVE RIGHT **The creek in Boston, Lincolnshire –** final resting place for large numbers of fishing boats.

RIGHT **The wreck of the** *Nornen*, a Norwegian barque driven ashore in 1897, on Berrow beach, Somerset. It is now thought to be a danger to jet skiers who want it blown up. Which would be a pity. This is a magical spot.

ABOVE The MV *Maanav Star* which went aground on 11 September 2004 at Jury's Gap near Camber, East Sussex. Not quite a wreck, but a close call.

LEFT Upturned boats used as fishermens' stores on the beach at Holy Island, Northumberland.

BELOW The wreck of the *Creteblock* on the beach at Whitby Scaur, North Yorkshire. This was one of the first concrete boats, built around 1919.

Lifeboats

The history of the lifeboat starts with the 'Unimmergible Boat' which was patented by Lionel Lukin in 1785. The sides of the boat were lined with cork and airtight cases.

We move swiftly on to Tynemouth and the two gentlemen associated with early lifeboats, Henry Greathead and William Wouldhave. The name of Greathead's craft was *The Lifeboat*, clearly a name more intelligible than Unimmergible.

BELOW *Tyne* – the second-oldest lifeboat in the country, built in 1833, South Shields, Tyne and Wear.

RIGHT The monument to Wouldhave and Greathead at South Shields, Tyne and Wear, also commemorates Queen Victoria's Golden Jubilee of 1887, as well as incorporating a drinking fountain, weathervane and clock.

Sir William Hillary was instrumental in setting up the Royal National Institution for the Preservation of Life from Shipwreck in 1824. The present-day RNLI is, of course, well known and respected. There are more than 300 lifeboats manned by over 4,000 volunteers and costing more than £280,000 a day to run.

A large number of lifeboat museums are dotted around the coast including the Grace Darling Museum at Bamburgh, the Zetland Museum at Redcar and the Henry Blogg Museum at Cromer.

ABOVE RIGHT **The Zetland Museum housed in the boathouse of 1877 on the esplanade at Redcar, North Yorkshire.**

RIGHT **The oldest lifeboat** *Zetland*, **a clinker-built rowing boat of 1802, built by Henry Greathead.**

ABOVE **The Lifeboat Inn pub sign at St Ives, Cornwall.**

RIGHT **The lifeboat** *Eric and Susan Hiscock (Wanderer)* **at Yarmouth, Isle of Wight.**

LEFT South Shields Volunteer Life Brigade Watch House of 1867, South Shields, Tyne and Wear.

BELOW The Life Brigade Watch House at Tynemouth, Tyne and Wear, built in 1886 by C T Gomoszynski.

LIFE BRIGADE WATCH HOUSE

LEFT The Rocket Garage at Cullercoats, Tyne and Wear, formerly the life brigade apparatus house dated 1867. The early brigades pioneered rocket life-lines. To the extreme left of the picture is a glimpse of the Police Box.

RIGHT The monument to the crew of the coble *Two Brothers* at Flamborough, East Yorkshire.

LEFT The Grace Darling National Memorial Museum at Bamburgh, Northumberland. Grace Darling (1815–42) was one of England's greatest heroines.

BELOW Inscription on the lifeboat obelisk at Southport, Merseyside.

Greater love hath no man

THIS MONUMENT
WAS ERECTED BY PUBLIC SUBSCRIPTIONS
TO COMMEMORATE THE CONSPICUOUS ACT
OF BRAVERY OF THE CREW OF THE COBLE
"TWO BROTHERS."
GEORGE GIBBON, MELCHOIR CHADWICK
THOMAS LENG MAJOR.
WHO GAVE THEIR LIVES IN A GALLANT
ATTEMPT TO SAVE THE CREW OF THE COBLE
"GLEANER."
JOHN CROSS HIS TWO SONS ROBERT CROSS
RICHARD MAJOR CROSS OF FLAMBOROUGH
WHO ALL PERISHED NEAR THE WEST SCAR
NORTH LANDING IN THE GREAT GALE
FEBRUARY 5TH 1909.

Will some kind hand please place a flower on this Obelisk in honour of all LIFEBOATMEN

HENRY BLOGG
G C BEM
COXSWAIN OF CROMER
LIFE-BOATS 1909-1947
WINNER OF THE R N L I
GOLD MEDAL
FOR CONSPICUOUS
GALLANTRY 3 TIMES
OF ITS SILVER MEDAL
4 TIMES
WITH THE HELP OF
HIS GALLANT CREW
RESCUED 873 LIVES
DURING 53 YEARS
OF SERVICE
·ONE OF THE
BRAVEST MEN
WHO EVER LIVED
DIED JUNE 13TH 1954

LEFT The bust of Henry Blogg at Cromer, Norfolk. He served as a lifeboatman for 53 years and his record of gallantry medals has not been surpassed.

RIGHT The lifeboat monument at St Anne's, Lancashire, 1890, commemorating the lifeboat men who lost their lives attempting to rescue the crew of the barque *Mexico*.

BELOW The RNLI monument at Lowestoft, Suffolk.

ABOVE **Caister-on-Sea lifeboat station, Norfolk. Famous for its record for most lives saved and for its motto 'Never turn back', it is now run independently from the RNLI.**

RIGHT **The former 1923 lifeboat shed from Cromer pier, Norfolk, now used as the Alfred Corry museum at Southwold, Suffolk, where the 1893 Southwold number 1 lifeboat is preserved.**

BELOW **The long jetty leading to the Bembridge lifeboat house on the Isle of Wight.**

War and peace

Waves of invaders, including marauding Vikings and Danes, have come ashore on the English coast but left few visible remains. Whizzing quickly through a thousand years of military and naval history, we might just spare a thought for the Cinque Ports, the Hundred Years War, the Tudor Navy, the Spanish Armada, the Anglo-Dutch Wars, the Battle of Trafalgar, the Great War, World War Two and, not least, the Cold War. All these have left their mark on the coast.

RIGHT **Dover Castle, Kent**, seen from the town. Set on a vital strategic site commanding the shortest sea crossing between England and the Continent, it boasts the longest history of any fortress in the country.

BELOW **Tilbury Fort, Essex.** The full panoply of martial might is displayed on the late 18th-century gatehouse.

ABOVE **Deal Castle, Kent. A Tudor artillery fortress.**

BELOW **Scarborough Castle, North Yorkshire.**

ABOVE **Bamburgh Castle, Northumberland.**

BELOW **Fort Perch, New Brighton, Merseyside.** Built in 1827 to defend the River Mersey.

ABOVE Garrison Point Fort, Sheerness Dockyard, Kent. Protecting the River Medway in conjunction with Grain Tower, the fort dates from the 1860s. To the lower left of the photograph the remains of the stanchions of the Brennan torpedo system can be seen.

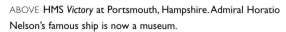

ABOVE HMS *Victory* at Portsmouth, Hampshire. Admiral Horatio Nelson's famous ship is now a museum.

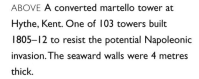

ABOVE A converted martello tower at Hythe, Kent. One of 103 towers built 1805–12 to resist the potential Napoleonic invasion. The seaward walls were 4 metres thick.

RIGHT Inscription on the side of the Trafalgar Memorial at Southsea, Hampshire. Controversy continues as to the exact wording of Nelson's signal on that fateful day of 21 October 1805. It has been suggested that Nelson actually said, 'England confides that every man will do his duty.'

ENGLAND EXPECTS EVERY MAN TO DO HIS DUTY.

ABOVE A ship's figurehead at Brightlingsea, Essex. Another Nelson conundrum. Is this a depiction of Nelson at some stage between the siege of Calvi, where he lost the use of one eye, and the battle of Santa Cruz where he lost his right arm? In fact, he may never have worn an eye-patch.

ABOVE A figurehead from HMS *Trafalgar*, a first-rate ship of 120 guns built in 1841, at the Royal Naval Dockyard, Portsmouth, Hampshire.

ABOVE A figurehead from HMS *Benbow*, a ship of 72 guns built in 1813, at the Royal Naval Dockyard, Portsmouth.

BELOW HMS *Warrior* at Portsmouth. Commissioned in 1861 as a three-masted sailing and steam ship, with a 'central citadel' iron box containing the main armament.

ABOVE LEFT The ubiquitous old cannon, this one is at Porthleven in Cornwall.

ABOVE The Collingwood memorial cannons at Tynemouth, Tyne and Wear. These are the original cannons from the *Royal Sovereign* which fought at the Battle of Trafalgar in 1805.

ABOVE A pill-box at Swanage, Dorset, probably predating the Second World War.

RIGHT The stark functionality of a concrete pill-box to the east of Coalhouse Fort at East Tilbury in Essex.

ABOVE **Coastal erosion at Happisburgh, Suffolk, has led to Second World War structures falling onto the beach.**

ABOVE **At Shellness beach in Kent.**

LEFT Dunkirk spirit on the New Welcome Sailor pub sign at Burnham on Crouch, Essex.

ABOVE An 'acoustic' or 'sound mirror' at Warden Point, Kent, now collapsed.

BELOW The concrete towers at Sheerness Dockyard in Kent.

ABOVE Operation Overlord slipways at Torquay, Devon. The 4th Infantry Division of the VII Corps of the United States 1st Army departed from here on 6 June 1944 for the D-Day landings.

RIGHT The 1914 Vickers pattern 13 PDR gun at Scarborough, North Yorkshire.

BELOW Between the hotels of the Grand Parade and the Redoubt Fortress Museum in Eastbourne, East Sussex, stands the 8th Hussars' Centurian tank 'Cameronian'.

LEFT Nelson's Monument at Great Yarmouth, Norfolk. Erected 1817–19, the figure of Britannia on the top is now a fibreglass replica.

ABOVE The statue of Sir Francis Drake at Plymouth, Devon, which was erected in 1884.

RIGHT **A detail of a panel on the side of the Ramsey Monument at Dover Castle, Kent, showing the Normandy landing.**

ABOVE **Monument to Admiral Sir Bertram Ramsay at Dover Castle, Kent. He was Commander-in-Chief Allied Naval Expeditionary Force, 1944.**

ABOVE **RAF Commonwealth and Allied Air Forces Second World War monument, Plymouth, Devon.**

ABOVE **The 'Yomper' Falklands Marine statue, Southsea, Hampshire.**

ABOVE The naval memorial at Portsmouth, Hampshire. Sir Robert Lorimer designed the First World War section, and the Second World War extension was the work of Sir Edward Maufe. There are 24,588 names on this monument.

RIGHT The Allen-Williams steel turret at Exmouth, Devon. Two men operated the turret, one to revolve it and one to fire a light machine gun.

BELOW The Boat Store at Sheerness Dockyard, Kent, 1856–60. An early surviving example of a multi-storey wrought-iron-frame building.

ABOVE **Dozens of mines are still to be found in seaside towns. This one is at Watchet, Somerset.**

LEFT **A black-painted sea mine at Dartmouth, Devon.**

RIGHT **A window in the Royal Garrison Church, Portsmouth, Hampshire, showing two 'Tommies'.**

Religion

George Bernard Shaw wrote: 'Heaven, as conventionally conceived, is a place so inane, so dull, so useless, so miserable, that nobody has ever ventured to describe a whole day in heaven, though plenty of people have described a day at the seaside.'

Much blessing of water, fish, boats, fishermen, throwing of crucifixes in the sea, 'beach preaching' and other more arcane religious ceremonies seem to take place round the coast. Seaside towns also seem to have a large number of churches. Whitby, for example, has Whitby Abbey, site of the Synod of Whitby, St Hilda's Church and the Caedmon Memorial, the English Martyrs' Church, the Evangelical Church, the Methodist Church, the New Life Church, Order of the Holy Paraclete, Our Lady's Church, St Anne's Church, St Bede's Church, St Hedda's Presbytery Church, St Patrick's Church, Trinity Church, West Cliff Congregational Church as well as any number of 'alternative religion' sites.

Religion is bewilderingly complicated. Let's hope our gods know what they are doing and talk to each other.

ABOVE **The replica Viking longboat** *Hugin* **built in 1949 by the Frederickssund Shipyard in Denmark and now at Pegwell Bay, Kent. The boat commemorates the landing of Hengist and Horsa in AD 49. They may have not been people but horse gods.**

RIGHT **The harbour wall at Lamorna Cove, Cornwall.**

ABOVE **Whitby Abbey, North Yorkshire, seen across the 'hard garden'.**

ABOVE RIGHT **The Bede Memorial Cross at Roker, Tyne and Wear.**

RIGHT **St Augustine's Cross at Minster, Kent.**

LEFT Doorway at Lindisfarne Priory, Holy Island, Northumberland – the site of one of the most important centres of Christianity in Anglo-Saxon England, founded in AD 635.

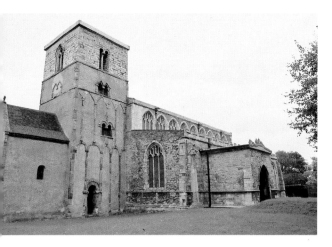

ABOVE The Saxon church of St Peter, Barton-upon-Humber, Lincolnshire. Dating from the 9th century, the tower has characteristic 'long and short work'.

ABOVE RIGHT The Sister Kirkes Memorial at Withernsea, East Yorkshire. The sea claimed St Mary's Church in 1444 and St Peter's Church at Owthorne by 1824.

BELOW The 'Twin Sisters' at Reculver, Kent. Dating to AD 669, the existing towers once had spires. These were erected in the 15th century on the orders of the Abbess of Faversham and her sister who had been shipwrecked off the Reculver coast. The main body of the church was demolished in 1809 but the towers were kept to aid navigation.

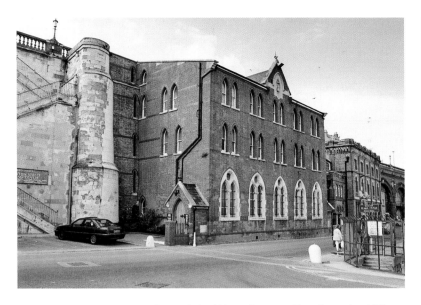

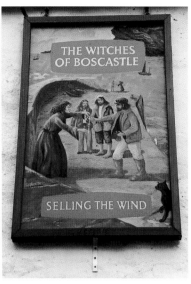

ABOVE The Sailors' Church and former Sailors' Home, Ramsgate, Kent. Opened in 1878, the dormitories at the top were provided for shipwreck survivors. To the right of the church is the Smack Boys' Home.

ABOVE The sign for the Witchcraft Museum at Boscastle, Cornwall.

BELOW Interior of the Sailors' Church.

LEFT The Sailors' and Fishermen's Bethel, Lowestoft, Suffolk.

BELOW The Sanger tombs at Margate cemetery, Kent, including the Mazeppa circus horse. The Sanger family were showmen and menagerists and developed the precursor of Dreamland, the Hall by the Sea.

Bathing

Towards the end of the 18th century, medicinal sea bathing had become popular with the gentry. Chalybeate springs and saline 'spa' water were thought to be a cure for melancholy, dyspepsia, catalepsy, nerves, etc. The colder the water the better. Bath houses and drinking wells later gave way to the new 'bathing machines' situated on the beach. The inter-war years saw further development. 'Bathing' turned into swimming and sunshine entered the equation and the era of the lido began. The popularity of Mediterranean holidays has led to the commercial marginalisation of cold water pools – except on the three hot days we get in an average English summer.

LEFT **The Royal Sea Bathing Hospital of 1791 at Margate, Kent.**

BELOW **Sea bathing in October at Eastbourne, East Sussex. Brrr!**

ABOVE The former bath house at Cromer, Norfolk. Built in 1814 as a subscription library, it later pumped sea water into private bath rooms.

RIGHT The mosaic sign for the Victoria Sea Water Baths of 1871, Southport, Merseyside.

BELOW Margate Lido, Kent, sadly now defunct – though the beacon survives.

LEFT Saltdean Lido, near Brighton, East Sussex, built in 1938 and still going strong.

ABOVE A mosaic sign advertising Lido Sands at Margate, Kent.

ABOVE The curvaceous paddling pool at Whitby, North Yorkshire.

LEFT The Art Deco Tinside Lido at Plymouth, Devon, which has recently been renovated.

ABOVE
Paddling pool on the esplanade at Whitley Bay, Tyne and Wear.

RIGHT Paddling pools at Amble by the Sea, Northumberland.

BELOW Paddling pool at Filey, North Yorkshire.

ABOVE Tynemouth paddling pool, Tyne and Wear. It appears to be a more hazardous place to paddle than the adjacent beach!

BELOW The Jubilee bathing pool at Penzance, Cornwall, 1935.

On the beach

Rocks and rock pools – good. Sands – good. Mud and quicksand – bad! That's pretty much it for beaches. I come from a family of inveterate beachcombers, so I do like a good tide line to walk along. There is, however, more and more plastic and globs of oil and sewage stuff to contend with. Busy beaches are for the kids to play together and mum and dad to read the newspaper. Deserted beaches are more for philosophising and/or walking dogs.

ABOVE **Sign on the side of Blands Corner Café in Scarborough, North Yorkshire.**

LEFT **The beach from the pier at Skegness, Lincolnshire.**

BELOW LEFT **A mural at Lyme Regis, Dorset.**

BELOW RIGHT **Life imitates art – a busy August day at Lyme Regis.**

ABOVE Sculptures in the sand at Weymouth, Dorset – the business started by the late Fred Darrington and now continued by Mark Anderson.

ABOVE A giant hippo sand sculpture at Scarborough, North Yorkshire.

ABOVE LEFT Picnic on the beach at Hornsea, East Yorkshire.

ABOVE A sandcastle on the beach at Newquay, Cornwall.

LEFT Paradise turned into a parking lot, Folkestone beach, Kent.

On the beach at Weymouth, Dorset.

Punch and Judy

Descending from the Italian Pulcinella and the Commedia dell 'Arte, Mr Punch is a trickster, jester and lord of misrule. He does bad things, is very frightening and small children love him. His nearest modern equivalent is the dalek. In France he is Polichinelle, in Germany he is Hans Wurst and in Russia, Petrushka. His props include a sausage, a ghost, a policeman, the devil, a crocodile and a big stick. So get out your swozzle and all shout: 'That's the way to do it!'.

RIGHT **Professor Des Turner at Herne Bay, Kent.**

BELOW **On the beach at Broadstairs, Kent.**

RIGHT **Professor Davey** at Lyme Regis, Dorset.

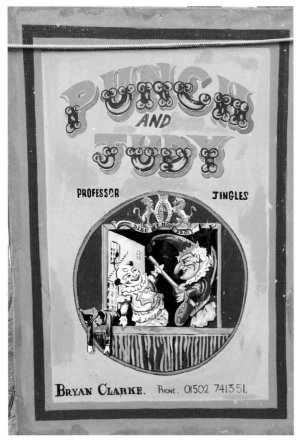

ABOVE **Professor Jingles at Herne Bay, Kent.**

ABOVE **Professor Jingles' sign.**

ABOVE **Professor David Wilde at Herne Bay, Kent.**

ABOVE **That's the way to do it!**

LEFT **Professor Felix at Herne Bay.**

BELOW **On the beach at Swanage, Dorset.**

Donkeys

Do donkeys know they are donkeys? They can, after all, interbreed with horses and zebras. A male donkey (known as a jackass) bred with a mare produces a mule, while the offspring of a stallion and a female donkey (called a jenny or jennet) is a hinny. You can, mostly, recognise a donkey by its long ears and characteristic 'Ee-aw' bray.

The first seaside resort to have donkey rides is thought to be Margate which introduced them around 1790. Donkeys at Blackpool now have workers' rights and work between 10am and 7pm, with Fridays off.

ABOVE **Enjoying 40 winks on the beach at Ramsgate, Kent, while waiting for the next customer.**

ABOVE **Two donkeys tuck into a hay net on a hot June day at Margate, Kent.**

ABOVE **'They're off!' – donkey rides at Skegness, Lincolnshire.**

LEFT **A cold day at the end of October on the sands at Scarborough, North Yorkshire.**

BELOW **On the beach at Margate, Kent.**

LEFT **Bells and bows bedeck these pretty donkeys posing near the pier at Cleethorpes, Lincolnshire.**

Piers

Defined as structures with decks built over water, piers can be functional for berthing vessels or, as is more common, for promenading and pleasure.

Ryde on the Isle of Wight appears to have the oldest pier built about 1814 for the landing of the ferry from the mainland. During the 19th century the developing resorts near London benefited from the paddle steamer services which provided popular 'day trips'. Arrival and departure were intermixed with promenading and 'taking the air' until commercial amusements became more organised. At the 'end of the pier' there might be an amusement arcade, or a camera obscura, or a cafe, or a theatre, or an aquarium, or a menagerie, or even a lifeboat station. The superstructure soon became more complex with pavilions, kiosks, shelters, seats, toilets and lighting. The piers at Ryde, Southend and Southport were so long they needed railways to get to the end.

Whilst we may have lost the West Pier at Brighton, all is not lost. The new pier at Southwold is a great success and there are 77 listed piers to visit.

BELOW **Wrought iron and timber seating along the Princess Pier at Torquay, Devon.**

ABOVE A sign for the Brighton Palace Pier, East Sussex.

RIGHT Worthing Pier, West Sussex, opened in 1862.

ABOVE Eastbourne Pier, East Sussex. This is usually voted the nation's favourite pier. Built in 1870 to a design by Eugenius Birch, it has an exotic mix of towers and turrets.

BELOW St Anne's Pier, Lancashire, opened in 1885.

LEFT Eastbourne Pier, East Sussex.

BELOW A cast iron gargoyle on Eastbourne Pier, painted blue like pretty much everything in Eastbourne.

LEFT Time you returned to the sanatorium. A glimpse of the Grand Pier at Weston super Mare, Somerset.

BELOW LEFT The remarkable entrance towers are all that remain of Withernsea Pier, East Yorkshire, 1877–1903.

BELOW The busy entrance of Clacton-on-Sea Pier, Essex, which was opened in 1871.

LEFT Cromer Pier, Norfolk, opened in 1900. Notice the Lifeboat Station at the end.

BELOW Paignton Pier, Devon, opened in 1879.

LEFT Not a seaside pier, but the wooden deck of HMS *Warrior*. Built in 1860, she now lies at Portsmouth, Hampshire.

LEFT Enjoying the pleasures of the North Pier at Blackpool, Lancashire, which opened to the public in 1863.

LEFT Skegness Pier, Lincolnshire. Opened in 1881, it quickly developed a thriving pleasure steamer service sailing from the pier across The Wash to Hunstanton where passengers could visit the Prince of Wales' estate at Sandringham.

LEFT Walton on the Naze Pier, Essex, 1895. The third longest pier with a marvellously complicated deck.

ABOVE Simple wooden seating on Cromer Pier, Norfolk.

BELOW Cast iron seating along Eastbourne Pier, East Sussex.

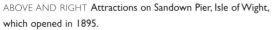

ABOVE AND RIGHT Attractions on Sandown Pier, Isle of Wight, which opened in 1895.

LEFT A screw pile from Bournemouth Pier, Dorset, now at the Amberley Museum, West Sussex.

RIGHT A decorative ironwork capital beneath the deck of the Cleethorpes Pier, Lincolnshire.

LEFT **A cautionary note at Eastbourne Pier, East Sussex.**

ABOVE **The sad remains of Brighton West Pier, East Sussex, in July 2003.**

BELOW **The paddle steamer *Waverley* approaching Margate Pier, Kent.**

The elegant Clevedon Pier in Somerset which was opened in 1869.
The arches are pairs of rails from a new rail system introduced by
Isambard Kindom Brunel to the South-West Railway but, when the
project failed, the track was uprooted.

Beach huts

What can be the origin of the beach hut? Some suggest that 'bathing machines' were re-used as changing rooms and then developed into picnic and sun rooms. Others maintain that fishermen's stores were taken over by holidaymakers. A surge in hut building happened in the post-war years when huts were cobbled together with whatever materials came to hand. Local authorities then stepped in to create order (ie rules) and to design, build and let out huts. Some huts even have residential status and overnight stays are possible as at Mudeford in Dorset. These command high prices – over £100,000.

If you like to sit in a musty, damp box full of yesterday's furniture and smelling of butane gas, listening to the rain on the roof and doing that wretched jigsaw with the missing piece, then this is for you. I salute the owner of Felixstowe's Beach Hut of the Year competition, first prize a china beach hut teapot. But there is a strange conflict in the world of the beach huts. They are quirky and individuals obviously try to personalise them but, at the same time, they are very samey and regimented. I want one.

BELOW **Hounsoms No 49 bathing machine on the beach at Eastbourne, East Sussex.**

ABOVE **A beach hut with tiny wheels near the pier at Southwold, Suffolk.**

ABOVE **A royal pair at Southwold.**

RIGHT 'West Winds Cottage' and 'Sheila's Cottage' – two large huts at Sandown, Isle of Wight.

BELOW Painting of Southwold, by Serena Hall, 1994.

BELOW 'Spunyarns' at Southwold.

ABOVE 'Forty Winks' at Southwold, Suffolk.

ABOVE 'Nuttahutta' at Whitstable, Kent.

ABOVE Infinite recession of huts at Bridlington, East Yorkshire.

ABOVE 'Thistledoo' at Brightlingsea, Essex.

ABOVE 'Forarest' at Walton on the Naze, Essex.

ABOVE What happens to huts in the winter at Southwold, Suffolk.

LEFT A splash of colour at Whitby, North Yorkshire.

BELOW LEFT Sign at Sandown, Isle of Wight.

BELOW Huts at Seaford, East Sussex.

BOTTOM Modern beach huts – part of the regeneration at Bridlington, East Yorkshire.

EASTERN BEACH CHALETS SANDOWN

EARLY SEASON REDUCTIONS

USE OF KITCHEN • TEA POT & CUPS • 3 DECK CHAIRS • TABLE CHAIRS • WINDBREAK • CLOSE TO TOILETS • DOUBLE DOORS PAVED PATIO • BEACH CAFE •

LEFT Beach
bungalows at
Fleetwood,
Lancashire.

BELOW
A curvaceous row
of Edwardian huts
at Scarborough,
North Yorkshire.

RIGHT **Garden** summerhouse style at Cowes, Isle of Wight.

BELOW **Pagoda**-shaped corrugated iron roofs at Mablethorpe, Lincolnshire.

ABOVE **'76 Trombones'** at Felixstowe, Suffolk.

LEFT **Innovative** beach huts at Hornsea, East Yorkshire.

ABOVE **Chalets at Filey, North Yorkshire.**

RIGHT **A home from home at Felixstowe, Suffolk.**

Cliff lifts

Lifts, trams, railways, funiculars, call them what you will, are a marvellous way to get from up there to down here and from down here to up there. Persons with a particular interest in lifts will like Scarborough where there have been no less than five lifts, the earliest dating from 1875. Another worthy lift is at Lynton and Lynmouth.

BELOW **The South Cliff Lift at Scarborough, North Yorkshire. Opened in 1875 and designed by Crossley Bros of Manchester, the lift used sea water as a counterweight.**

ABOVE **The Central Tramway at Scarborough, North Yorkshire, dating to 1881. Designed originally for steam, it was converted to electricity in 1910.**

BELOW Sign for the Central Tramway at Scarborough.

ABOVE East Hill Lift at Hastings, East Sussex, built in 1903.

BELOW The lift at Shanklin, Isle of Wight. A vertical hydraulic lift was built in 1891 and replaced by an enclosed concrete tower lift in 1956.

ABOVE Saltburn-by-the-Sea, North Yorkshire, looking down towards the pier.

RIGHT Sign at Saltburn-by-the-Sea.

Hotels

You can pour over brochures, agonise over hundreds of little pictures of samey-looking hotels and guest houses – and still seem to get it wrong. The answer often lies in the name. 'Hotels' seem to be anonymous while 'guest houses' seem to imply that you will be treated as a guest and be properly looked after. Very large seaside hotels can often be swamped by coach parties – I can recall being thrown aside at breakfast at a Newquay establishment by the surge to get to the crispy bacon. The very small amateur establishment can be friendly, but this can sometimes be a problem if the owners want to know all about you and insist that you sit in their lounge and entertain them. Beware of places with too many rules and regulations – 'No baths on Mondays', 'No more than two persons in the shower at one time' and 'If you touch the twin bed you are not using, you will have to pay for it'. I really dislike those 'breakfast choice cards' you have to fill in the night before, itemising what you must eat in the morning. And also don't you just hate being put at a breakfast table with strangers? However, we mustn't carp. More often than not you will find a safe haven and you are there to see the sea, not the bedrooms. (Incidentally, does anybody actually use those trouser presses?)

BELOW **Palatial Victorian opulence at the Grand Hotel in Brighton, East Sussex. This five-star hotel was built on the seafront in 1864.**

ABOVE The elegant Brighton Metropole Hotel, built in 1890 to designs by Alfred Waterhouse, the architect of the Natural History Museum in London.

ABOVE The Metropole Arts Centre, Folkestone, Kent. Formerly the New Metropole Hotel, 1895.

RIGHT The Grand Hotel, Scarborough, North Yorkshire. Built in 1863–7 and designed by Cuthbert Brodrick, this immense structure dominates the town.

BELOW The Palace Hotel, Paignton, Devon. The former home of Washington Singer, son of Sir Isaac Singer, the inventor of the sewing machine.

BELOW RIGHT The Grand Hotel at New Brighton, Merseyside. Not to be confused with the Grand Hotel, Brighton, East Sussex.

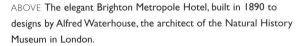

ABOVE **Hotels on the Eastern Esplanade at Paignton, Devon.**

RIGHT **The romantic House in the Sea, Newquay, Cornwall, complete with its own suspension bridge.**

BELOW **Court Royal, Bournemouth, Dorset. Formerly the Madeira Hotel where Marconi received the first paid radio message in 1898, it is now a miners' convalescent home.**

BELOW RIGHT **The Grosvenor House Hotel at Skegness, Lincolnshire, incorporates a café, chemist and, amazingly, a ballroom.**

RIGHT
The Wellington Hotel at Boscastle, Cornwall. Pictured before the great flood of 2004, this hotel has 17th-century origins but was rebuilt in 1853.

BELOW The Pink Beach Hotel, Shanklin, Isle of Wight.

LEFT Franklin Hotel at Blackpool. A typical 'three lamper'.

LEFT Willow Grove Hotel, Blackpool, Lancashire. The usual three lamps in the window here replaced by a tiger with cubs.

LEFT Bed and breakfast at Blackpool.

BELOW Typical bed and breakfast establishments in Blackpool.

ABOVE Central Spa Hotel, Blackpool. A 'three lamper' at night.

BELOW The Howard Hotel, Blackpool. A 'four lamper' at night.

BELOW The Xoron Floatel at Bembridge, Isle of Wight. An ex-World War Two motor gun-boat with a guest lounge over 27 metres in length.

Wooden walls

Miscellaneous wooden buildings dot the coast. Often these are clinker built or constructed from salvage, while others are re-used railway carriages. These buildings are often places created by free spirits who don't like the regimentation of beach huts or chalets or caravans.

RIGHT **A houseboat at Shoreham by Sea, West Sussex.**

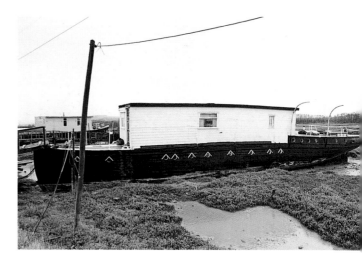

LEFT **A new age houseboat at Shoreham by Sea.**

BELOW **Marconi Laboratory at Dungeness, Kent.**

LEFT **Houses directly on the beach at Shellness, Isle of Sheppey, Kent.**

RIGHT **The veranda.**

ABOVE 'Waveland', Sutton on Sea, Lincolnshire. A stack of four railway carriages built about 1908.

LEFT 'Half Sovereign Cottage' on the Stade at Hastings, East Sussex.

BELOW 'Lindum', Sutton on Sea. Built from two railway carriages.

LEFT Hut with portholes to the side of 'The Beach House', Whitstable, Kent.

BELOW 'Leven', Dungeness, Kent. A former railway carriage.

ABOVE The Edwardian sail lofts or yacht stores at Tollesbury, Essex.

RIGHT Beach lookout at Hurst Spit, Hampshire.

Caravans and chalets

Love them or hate them? You cannot be indifferent. Many people dislike caravans and we try to hide them away behind trees and fences. But loads of people cannot afford, or don't want, to stay at opulent grand hotels or middle-sized hotels, or even a humble B&B. Renting a caravan can get you out of the city and onto the beach.

RIGHT **Sand Bay caravan park sign at Kewstoke, Somerset.**

ABOVE **The caravan park at Winchelsea Beach, East Sussex.**

LEFT **Redcar Beach caravan park, North Yorkshire, with Billingham oil refinery in the distance.**

ABOVE **Caravans at Lowestoft, Suffolk.**

ABOVE **Chalets at West Bay, Bridport, Dorset.**

ABOVE **The 1954 Airstream caravan outside 'Vista', the rubber-clad beach house designed by Simon Conder at Dungeness, Kent.**

ABOVE RIGHT **Chalets dating from the 1930s at Eden Leisure Park, Leysdown-on-Sea, Kent.**

RIGHT **More chalets at Leysdown-on-Sea.**

Seaside architecture of the 1930s

The 1930s was a period when buildings began to mirror the clean lines of ocean liners, when 'form was to follow function'. The origin of this style of architecture is firmly rooted in the Bauhaus tradition and it is no surprise to find many European architects working in England – including Erich Mendelsohn, Serge Chermayeff and Berthold Lubetkin.

The 1930s buildings to be seen at the seaside usually have masses of white-painted concrete, flat roofs and metal windows. With all the ingredients for decay when subjected to sand, sea and salt, most of the larger structures are under constant repair.

ABOVE **The RIBA medal awarded to the RCYC in 1931.**

RIGHT **The Royal Corinthian Yacht Club at Burnham on Crouch, Essex. Designed in 1931 by Joseph Emberton.**

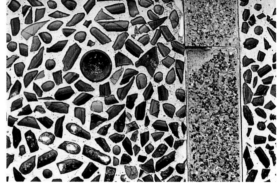

ABOVE **'Bottle Alley',** Hastings, East Sussex. The lower deck of the 'double-decker' sea front promenade built in the early 1930s by the 'Concrete King' Sidney Little.

LEFT **A detail of the broken bottles in 'Bottle Alley'.**

ABOVE The De La Warr Pavilion at Bexhill-on-Sea, East Sussex, which was designed by Mendelsohn and Chermayeff and built in 1935.

BELOW The Labworth Café at Canvey Island, Essex, which was built by Ove Arup in 1933.

LEFT 'New Haven', Herne Bay, Kent. Map evidence shows it was built pre-1939.

RIGHT The Midland Hotel, Morecambe, Lancashire. Built by the LMS Railway in 1932–3 to the design of Oliver Hill, with interior details by Eric Gill and Eric Ravilious.

BELOW The entrance to 'New Haven'.

LEFT The 1930s chic corkscrew tower of Blackpool Pleasure Beach 'New Casino' entrance, Lancashire.

BELOW Worthing Pier, West Sussex. Rebuilt in modernist style after a fire in 1933.

ABOVE An 'Oyster' bungalow at Beachlands estate, Pevensey, East Sussex, dating to the late 1930s.

RIGHT Royal Birkdale Golf Club, Southport, Merseyside, 1935.

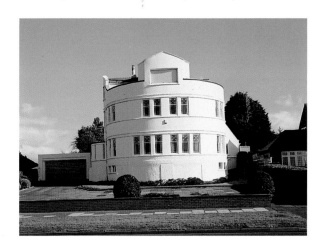

ABOVE 'The Roundhouse', Southport.

ABOVE 'The Round House' at Frinton-on-Sea, Essex.

Shelters

The shelter is the most widespread and diverse architectural feature of the seaside yet it is largely unnoticed and unappreciated. Few shelters are listed or dated and we will never know the names of their designers. In times of cutbacks they receive little or no maintenance, regeneration schemes often sweep them away and they are also prone to vandalism. Enjoy these little gems while you can.

ABOVE
The wonderful rock-cut shelter at Polperro, Cornwall.

LEFT A massive shelter dated 1891 at Plymouth, Devon.

BELOW LEFT
A thatched shelter at North Lodge Park, Cromer, Norfolk.

BELOW Bandstand style at St Anne's, Lancashire. Note the gas lamp and a glimpse of the cast iron esplanade wall.

ABOVE An example of a roofless wind shelter at Saltburn-by-the-Sea, North Yorkshire.

ABOVE RIGHT The Rockcliffe Bowling Club shelter at Whitley Bay, Tyne and Wear. The right-hand side seats face the bowling green and the left-hand seats face the sea. A similar arrangement exists at the Island Wall Tennis Club in Whitstable, Kent.

RIGHT A grand masonry shelter at Scarborough, North Yorkshire.

BELOW The sign in the Mundesley shelter.

ABOVE Walk through at Southsea, Hampshire.

ABOVE A shelter at Mundesley, Norfolk.

ABOVE **Scarborough, North Yorkshire.**

ABOVE **The 'United States Navy' shelter at Fowey, Cornwall.**

ABOVE **The Blackpool pagoda-like style of about 1905.**

ABOVE **Massive tiled roof at Cromer, Norfolk.**

ABOVE **The extraordinary little blue painted shelters at Trusville, Trusthorpe, Lincolnshire.**

ABOVE **A shelter in the Connaught Gardens, Sidmouth, Devon.**

ABOVE King's Parade, New Brighton, Merseyside.

ABOVE A shelter at Southsea, Hampshire.

ABOVE High Victoriana at Southend-on-Sea, Essex.

ABOVE A shelter built on stilts at Southend-on-Sea, Essex.

ABOVE The large western shelter at Margate, Kent – a structure of great complexity.

ABOVE Summerhouse style at Scarborough, North Yorkshire.

ABOVE Shelter at Spittal beach near Berwick-upon-Tweed, Northumberland, dated 1930.

ABOVE 1960s style at Prince of Wales Pier, Dover, Kent.

ABOVE New shelters at Dover, Kent.

ABOVE The reconstructed Lowry shelter at Berwick-upon-Tweed, Northumberland.

ABOVE **A 1930s shelter at Margate, Kent.**

ABOVE **Regeneration at Bridlington, East Yorkshire.**

ABOVE **Domed shelters at Lowestoft, Suffolk.**

ABOVE **The 'Art Nouveau' shelter at Southport, Merseyside.**

ABOVE **An example from Weymouth, Dorset.**

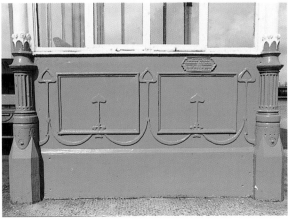

ABOVE **Detail of the 'Art Nouveau' shelter.**

Telephone kiosks

Although around 2,000 kiosks have 'listed building' status, it is an incontrovertible fact that very few people use them. They are however quintessentially English and are part of the fabric of the seaside environment.

ABOVE The more usual K6 kiosk of 1924. This one is at the top of Blackpool Tower, Lancashire.

ABOVE A rare example of the K1 designed by Giles Gilbert Scott in 1921, standing in the High Street at Bembridge, Isle of Wight.

RIGHT A K6 virtually on the beach at Budleigh Salterton, Devon.

ABOVE **Nautical flavour at Paignton Harbour, Devon.**

ABOVE RIGHT **A blue painted kiosk at Ramsgate, Kent.**

LEFT **The distinctive white painted kiosks at Hull, East Yorkshire.**

RIGHT **A rare 'Tardis' Police telephone box at Scarborough, North Yorkshire.**

Something to sit on

Deckchairs

Usually found corralled in piles on the beach with deckchair attendants not in attendance. Other chairs are seemingly abandoned, their occupants having given up and gone for a cuppa. The old cotton versions have long given way to nylon, but the traditional stripes remain. Some resorts even have their own colour codes. One of life's small pleasures is watching someone struggling to put up a deckchair in the wind.

Solid seats

Seats are made from a multiplicity of materials – cast iron, wood, stainless steel, plastic, concrete, you name it. Lots of seats seem to commemorate those who sat there in their favourite place staring out to sea. Designers and manufacturers are usually anonymous and perhaps we are not really meant to notice a well placed seat, especially if we are sitting on it.

BELOW **On the front at Brighton, East Sussex.**

RIGHT Looking towards the pier at Sandown, Isle of Wight.

ABOVE On the pier at Bournemouth, Dorset.

LEFT Waiting for customers at Lyme Regis, Dorset.

ABOVE **A cast-iron seat at Ventnor, Isle of Wight.**

ABOVE **The Edith Cavell seat at Hunstanton, Norfolk.**

LEFT
The extraordinary long seat at Bridlington, East Yorkshire.

RIGHT Stainless steel at Hornsea, East Yorkshire.

ABOVE **At Corbyn Head, Torquay, Devon.**

ABOVE **The next seat along.**

ABOVE 'Unsitonable' seat at Scarborough, North Yorkshire.

ABOVE Chocolate brown 1970s look at Scarborough, North Yorkshire. Uncomfortable, but what a classic.

ABOVE Withernsea, East Yorkshire.

ABOVE Regeneration at Skegness, Lincolnshire.

113

ABOVE **A poetical seat and table at Hunstanton, Norfolk.**

RIGHT **Hippopotamus seat at Bridlington, East Yorkshire.**

LEFT **Regeneration at South Shore Promenade, Bridlington, by the architectural practice of Bauman Lyons with artist Bruce McLean.**

RIGHT **Sandcastle-seats at Whitley Bay, Tyne and Wear.**

RIGHT
Ammonite seats at
Whitby, North
Yorkshire.

Public conveniences

Often combined with shelters or bandstands, these buildings of lowly status are frequently disregarded and subject to vandalism and neglect. Few original interiors remain.

BELOW **The Promenade conveniences dated 1937, at Paignton, Devon.**

RIGHT Gentlemen's public convenience *c* 1905 at Bournemouth, Dorset.

ABOVE **Late 19th-century cast iron decoration in the disused public conveniences at Margate, Kent.**

ABOVE **The bandstand with conveniences below, at South Shields, Tyne and Wear.**

ABOVE **Public conveniences beneath the large shelter, South Shields, Tyne and Wear.**

ABOVE The conveniences at Felixstowe, Suffolk.

RIGHT Conveniences at Southport, Merseyside, with stained glass and timber framing. Flowers and lace curtains are an added attraction, and an attendant is on call.

BELOW Railings surround the underground facilities at Weymouth, Dorset.

Contemporary seaside sculpture

Unfortunately, the British public does not, as a rule, take to contemporary sculpture. But what is art but an attempt to improve surroundings, to stimulate the passer-by to ask questions, to challenge?

RIGHT **The Henry Moore sculpture at Snape Maltings, Suffolk. I think we can award it 'seaside status' as the visitors to Snape generally stay at the seaside.**

LEFT **'Epidauros' by Barbara Hepworth at Pedn Olva, St Ives, Cornwall.**

BELOW **'Sea Music' by Sir Anthony Caro at Poole, Dorset.**

LEFT **'Scallop' by Maggi Hambling at Aldeburgh, Suffolk, which has suffered from vandalism.**

RIGHT 'Conversation Piece' by Juan Munoz, 1999, at South Shields, Tyne and Wear.

RIGHT 'They shoot horses don't they?' by Michael Trainor, 2002. The world's largest mirror ball. Blackpool, Lancashire.

ABOVE 'Lunar Pieces', seven phases of the moon set in concrete bowls by Chaz Brenchley at Roker beach, Sunderland, Tyne and Wear.

RIGHT 'On the crest of a wave' by Ray Smith, 1996, at Dover, Kent.

BELOW Where decorative art meets sculpture? Railings at Bournemouth, Dorset, with bucket and spade.

RIGHT 'Family of Penguins' by Tony Wiles, 1994, at Redcar, North Yorkshire. The penguins are looking at another work, 'Picture Postcard Railings' by Chris Topp.

ABOVE 'Whalebone' by Reece Ingrams, at Herne Bay, Kent – a sculpture very popular with children.

ABOVE Another children's favourite – 'The Treasure Chest' by Nigel Hobbins, at Herne Bay, Kent.

ABOVE Barbara Hepworth's studio at St Ives, Cornwall.

Seaside gardens

Municipal seaside parks and gardens seem to have been in decline for some years. A stroll along the prom will often reveal a general contraction of flower bed area and an increase in lawn area. But, though there may be fewer flower beds, there are still loads left to provoke plenty of 'oohs' and 'aahs' at their bright and brash splashes of colour.

At Southport, for example, there is the classic Botanic Gardens, the British Lawn Mower Museum, Hesketh Park with its wooded lakeland setting, Rotten Row – an internationally renowned flower bed, King's Gardens, the aptly named Floral Hall and, not least, Victoria Park, the home of the Southport Flower Show. Unlike the colder and windy east coast, Southport enjoys a balmy Gulf-Stream kind of weather ideal for growing sub-tropical and Mediterranean plants.

ABOVE **Lamplit walk at Southport, Merseyside.**

BELOW **A flower-filled dinghy at Tynemouth, Tyne and Wear.**

ABOVE **Floral display at Skegness, Lincolnshire.**

RIGHT **The sunken garden on the esplanade at Whitley Bay, Tyne and Wear.**

BELOW The Roman Stones in a circular bed at Filey, North Yorkshire.

ABOVE Strange little beds at Cleethorpes, Lincolnshire.

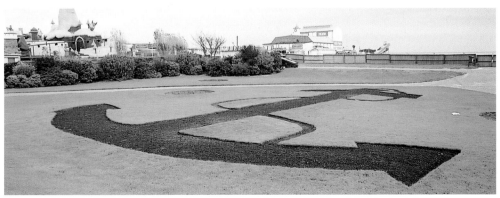

ABOVE A circular bed awaiting planting at Dawlish, Devon.

LEFT A giant anchor flower bed at Great Yarmouth, Norfolk.

123

RIGHT Barbara
Hepworth's
sculpture garden at
St Ives, Cornwall.

BELOW Pulhamite
rockery at
Ramsgate, Kent.

ABOVE In the 'Axenstrasse' at Skegness, Lincolnshire.

BELOW The Gertrude Jekyll walled garden, created in 1911 at Lindisfarne Castle, Northumberland.

RIGHT The shell grotto at Gyllyngdune Gardens, Falmouth, Cornwall.

ABOVE 'Prospect Cottage', the former home of Derek Jarman, at Dungeness, Kent.

ABOVE Flotsam and jetsam at the 'Venus of Dungeness' garden.

ABOVE The 'Venus of Dungeness' garden, Dungeness, Kent.

ABOVE **The Broad Walk yew hedge at Walmer Castle, Kent.**

ABOVE **A floral fish at Sidmouth, Devon.**

RIGHT **A houseboat garden at Bembridge, Isle of Wight.**

Model villages

Generally speaking the models tend to be rather stuck in time. They also seem to reflect the interests, if not obsessions, of their originators. Twee, yes, often sentimental, they are still intriguing, amusing and delightful. What we are most sensitive to is the slightest discrepancy of scale. 'Lands of the little people' are also to be found at Blackpool, Great Yarmouth, Corfe Castle, Babbacombe and Portsmouth.

ABOVE LEFT
Sign for the Ramsgate Model Village, Kent. Built in 1953, it is now sadly closed.

ABOVE Ramsgate Model Village.

LEFT Little and large at the Ramsgate Model Village.

RIGHT
A dilapidated model castle at Never Never Land, Southend-on-Sea, Essex.

ABOVE W E Slapiton at work in the Skegness Model Village.

ABOVE Semore Clearly and Lucy Lastic at Skegness Model Village.

BELOW Skegness Model Village, Lincolnshire.

Bandstands

How wonderful to come across a bandstand with a band playing! Usually they seem abandoned and unloved. Perhaps we might not go as far as believing they are the sites of ancient worship, at the hub of ley lines and infused with magical healing power, but they are fun and often exuberantly decorated and embellished, full of chutzpah and civic pride.

RIGHT **The recently erected bandstand in Crescent Gardens, Filey, North Yorkshire.**

ABOVE **Deckchairs surround the Central bandstand at Eastbourne, East Sussex, built in 1935.**

ABOVE **Looking up at the Bedford Square bandstand of 1884 at Brighton, East Sussex. Now marooned atop the public conveniences.**

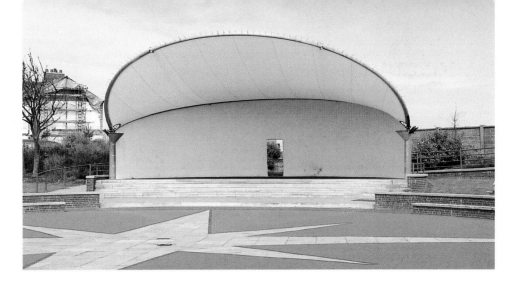

RIGHT **Tented bandstand at Withernsea, East Yorkshire.**

BELOW **Dated 1907, the Gyllyngdune Gardens bandstand at the Princess Pavilion complex, Falmouth, Cornwall. Lush vegetation threatens to hide the brass band.**

Amusements

Arcades, pleasure domes, sideshows, ghosts and ghouls, crazy houses, laughing clowns, a peppering of the surreal, the unusual and the bizarre…all the fun of the fair and all the fun of the beach rolled into one. The very names of the rides – Hypercoaster, Twister, Whip, Big Dipper, River Caves, Iceblast, Valhalla – invite us to let our hair down and jump into the other world of brash colour and loud music. We can also find plenty of smaller amusements – Hook a Duck, Mr Blobby, Postman Pat and an infinite variety of slot machines. I particularly like those shove-penny ones.

Old rides abound. At Margate you will still see the Scenic Railway of 1920; at Blackpool the Grand National of 1934 and the Flying Machine of 1904;

ABOVE **The Kursaal at Southend-on-Sea, Essex, 1898–9. Formerly 26 acres** of amusements including a menagerie.

at Great Yarmouth the Scenic Railway of 1932 and at Southport the Cyclone of 1937. The great rides and all the brouhaha, coloured lights and flash bang wallop are, of course, not there for your education and benefit but to take your money.

So, roll up, roll up, and bring plenty of change. You will need it!

ABOVE
Charles Mannings'
Amusements,
Felixstowe, Suffolk,
1945.

LEFT Spanish City,
Whitley Bay, Tyne
and Wear, opened
in 1910 as a
pleasure dome and
ballroom.

ABOVE Dreamland Amusement Park, Margate, Kent, 1920. Seen here is the main front in 1994.

ABOVE Caesar's Fun Palace at Great Yarmouth, Norfolk. We can only imagine what the original Caesar would make of this!

LEFT The typical 'Plaza' amusements at Skegness, Lincolnshire.

LEFT All the family is welcome at Silver City Amusements at Cleethorpes, Lincolnshire.

LEFT Circus Circus at the Yarmouth Hippodrome, Great Yarmouth, Norfolk. Built in 1903 as 'the finest palace of entertainment in Great Britain' and now home to 'Circus Hilarious'.

RIGHT Amusements on the beach at Margate, Kent.

ABOVE The sign on the Central Beach Office at Sandown Isle of Wight.

ABOVE Amusements on the beach at Ramsgate, Kent.

ABOVE
Rollercoaster at Skegness,
Lincolnshire.

ABOVE RIGHT
Luna Park Amusements at
Scarborough, North Yorkshire.

BELOW
The Cyclone, opened in 1937
at Pleasureland, Southport,
Merseyside.

RIGHT
The Runaway Coaster of 1922
at Rotunda Amusement Park,
Folkestone, Kent.

ABOVE **A rollercoaster of 1934 vintage – The Grand National at Blackpool, Lancashire.**

ABOVE **Fantasy Island, Skegness, Lincolnshire.**

ABOVE **The Crazy House at Dymchurch Amusements, Kent.**

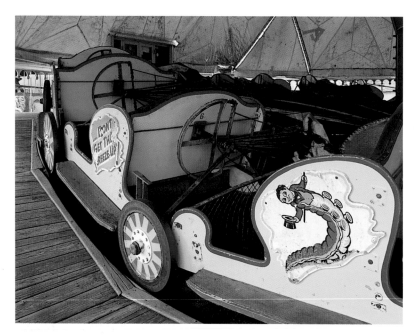

ABOVE The Ghost Train at Pleasureland, Southport, Merseyside.

LEFT The Caterpillar at Pleasureland, Southport, dating from 1914.

BELOW Arcades come into their own at night. Funland Amusements, Blackpool, Lancashire.

ABOVE **Mr B's** welcomes you to the 'Golden Mile' at Blackpool, Lancashire.

LEFT **The Crazy Clown** ride at Brighton, East Sussex.

ABOVE A Silver Sails pinball machine found abandoned in a field near Bristol.

LEFT A Passion Tester machine at Scarborough, North Yorkshire.

RIGHT A Mr Muscle machine at Clacton-on-Sea, Essex.

LEFT **Tick-Tock** and Fruit-Bowl, two older-style machines at Mablethorpe, Lincolnshire.

RIGHT The Tim Hunkin 'Doctor' machine at Southwold, Suffolk. Scary.

LEFT Bingo at Scarborough, North Yorkshire.

BELOW The laughing clown always has the last laugh. Fleetwood, Lancashire.

Helter-skelters

Once one of the icons of the seaside amusement park, the old-style helter-skelters are fast disappearing. Only about three or four remain at the seaside although two have found their way to museums – one at the Black Country Museum at Dudley and one at the Hollicombe Steam Museum at Liphook.

The helter-skelter was probably first introduced by travelling fairs in the late 19th century. Early postcard views are unusual, although I have seen one from Cleethorpes dated 1902, one from Southport dated 1905 and one from the New Zealand International Exhibition of 1906.

Although they now seem staid and slow compared with the rollercoasters, they must have seemed pretty exciting at one time. Huge parallel 'astraglide' switchback rides have superseded the humble helter-skelter, although new-style, temporary, open-framework helter-skelters are sometimes found on the beach, as at Weymouth.

BELOW **The Rotunda Amusement Park at Folkestone, Kent, before its closure.**

ABOVE **Pleasureland, Southport, Merseyside.**

RIGHT **Outside Butlins at Minehead, Somerset.**

BELOW **Dreamland, Margate, Kent.**

RIGHT
The 'Dutch Tutch' at Potter Heigham, Norfolk. Rescued from the Great Yarmouth Pier, Norfolk, after a fire in 1914, and re-erected as a house.

BELOW
Hunstanton, Norfolk.

RIGHT
On the Palace Pier, Brighton, East Sussex.

BELOW
Southend-on-Sea, Essex.

Carousels

These colourful fairground rides have many names – 'whirligigs', 'roundabouts', 'merry-go-rounds', 'gallopers', 'manèges de chevaux de bois', and are often found at the seaside. They have their origins in 17th-century French tournaments where horsemen tilted at brass rings. Subsequently, legless wooden horses were attached to a rotating platform and contestants had to ride these and attempt to spear stationary rings. The carousel revolved anti-clockwise to allow the right arm to carry the lance but, as this game never developed in England, English carousels revolve clockwise. By the late 19th century two Englishmen, Frederick Savage and Robert Tidman, developed steam-powered carousels and added to the appeal of the ride with the introduction of an up-and-down galloping motion. Early steam carousels can sometimes be recognised by their chimneys.

ABOVE
The carousel at Pleasureland, Southport, Merseyside.

ABOVE RIGHT
June, Ela and Sid gallop around the carousel at Folkestone, Kent.

RIGHT
The Venetian Carousel on North Pier, Blackpool, Lancashire. Notice that the horses go anti-clockwise.

ABOVE English Victorian Galloping Horses at Bournemouth, Dorset.

BELOW The magnificent Tommy Matthews Galloping Horses on the beach at Brighton, East Sussex.

Golf

The world-famous golf course at St Andrews in Scotland was reputedly formed by sheep closely cropping the fairways and developing handy bunkers in which to shelter from the wind. It is thought that the word 'golf' is derived from the German word 'kolbe', meaning 'club'. The names of many of the clubs used by the players sound strange to the ear: 'brassies', 'spoons', 'cleeks', 'mashies' and 'niblicks'. To non-golfers, the rest of the terminology is well nigh incomprehensible: 'par', 'birdie', 'triple bogey'.

There seems to be a difference between 'golf courses' and 'golf links'. Links are found beside the sea and are basically sand dunes with long-rooted short grass. Links courses are well drained and you don't get your feet muddy.

Crazy golf is another iconic seaside resort amusement. It also comes with a wide range of names and rules. There is a difference between 'crazy golf' and 'adventure golf' and between 'miniature golf' and 'minigolf'. Crazy golf seems to originate with the game of 'golfstacle', a form of 'garden golf' popular around 1910. There is also 'clock golf' and 'pitch and putt'.

BELOW **A naïve oil painting of Royal St George's Golf Club at Sandwich, Kent.**

ABOVE
'Linkscape' at Royal St George's.

LEFT
One of the thatched shelters at Royal St George's.

ABOVE **Crazy golf at Skegness, Lincolnshire.**

ABOVE **Crazy golf at Eastern Esplanade, Southend-on-Sea, Essex.**

ABOVE **Pitch and putt at Filey, North Yorkshire.**

ABOVE **Interplanetary golf at Bridlington, East Yorkshire.**

LEFT **Crazy golf on Weymouth beach, Dorset.**

Food

A typical meal at the seaside will consist of fish and chips and a pot of tea followed by apple pie and custard. For a bit of a change, you could go for the all-day breakfast or something simple like sausage, egg and chips or beans on toast (incidentally, the 'full English breakfast' should include nine items!). Nearer to London, you might find eel pie and mash. 'Local' seafood can be enjoyed all round the coast: Cromer crabs, Whitstable oysters, Morecambe Bay shrimps…. Alternatively, you might decide to go for a 'Chinese', an 'Indian', or an 'Italian'. Some seaside towns aspire to haute cuisine and cordon bleu designer bistros in Mediterranean style, with patio heaters and London prices. We are lucky that there is such diversity of food on offer in such amazing surroundings. However, we must lament the loss of so many Formica, Bakelite and chrome 50s and 60s 'coffee bars', especially the York Gate Café interior at Broadstairs. It's also a shame that the candyfloss machines seem to have disappeared. You can still buy candyfloss but it comes in a plastic bag with no stick and it's just not the same.

LEFT
One of the larger cafés at Minehead, Somerset.

BELOW
Ice cream parlour at Birchington, Kent. Ice cream parlours are few and far between.

ABOVE Sign at Blackpool, Lancashire.

LEFT Pie, mash and liquor on offer at Leysdown-on-Sea, Kent.

ABOVE
Interior of the ice cream parlour at Birchington, Kent.

ABOVE RIGHT
Interior of Pantrinis Café at Whitley Bay, Tyne and Wear.

RIGHT
The Leaking Boot Restaurant and Chippie at Cleethorpes, Lincolnshire. Notice the fibreglass pugilistic chef.

RIGHT
Henry's Beach
Shop at Sandown,
Isle of Wight.

BELOW
Fast food at
Minehead,
Somerset.

ABOVE **Burger bar at Skegness, Lincolnshire.**

ABOVE **The Intrepid Bun at Southsea, Hampshire.**

ABOVE **The ruined burger bar at Ainsdale beach, Merseyside.**

RIGHT The fish and chip shop at California, Norfolk.

BELOW Chalkboard advertisement for cones of chips at Worthing, West Sussex.

ABOVE Fish and chips at Broadstairs, Kent.

RIGHT Essential condiments for fish and chips in the pier café at Southend-on-Sea, Essex.

ABOVE Sign at Scarborough, North Yorkshire.

LEFT A long-established fish and chip shop at Blackpool, Lancashire. Despite its 1950s exterior, inside it has the feel of the 1930s.

ABOVE An ice cream parlour at Scarborough, North Yorkshire bearing the famous name of the Pacitto family. The Italian connection with ice cream goes back to the mid-19th century when Italian ice cream vendors known as 'Hokey Pokey' men toured major cities. The name derives from their cry of 'Oche poco' meaning 'Oh so cheap'.

LEFT Painted sign at the Rendezvous Café, Whitley Bay, Tyne and Wear.

RIGHT The Askeys' ice cream cone girl in the window of an ice cream parlour at Birchington, Kent.

LEFT The Bigtop cone at Macaris Restaurant at Herne Bay, Kent.

RIGHT The Facchino ice cream cone girl at Fusciardi's Ice Cream Tea and Coffee Lounge at Eastbourne, East Sussex.

BELOW A large '99' cone on the beach at Ramsgate, Kent.

ABOVE Mick's Super Softy ice cream van at Canvey Island, Essex.

ABOVE Carlo's ice cream van at Tynemouth, Tyne and Wear.

RIGHT The Scooby and Shaggy ice cream van at Margate, Kent.

BELOW Mister Softee ice cream van at Silloth on Solway, Cumbria.

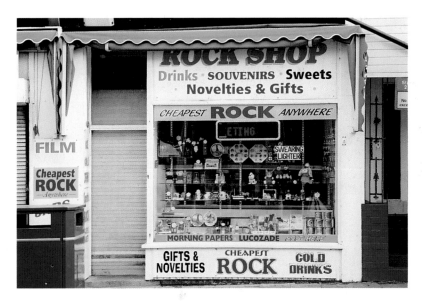

ABOVE **The cheapest rock anywhere, Blackpool, Lancashire.**

BELOW **Rock of all sizes and shapes at Blackpool, Lancashire.**

RIGHT **John Bull Rockmakers, Scarborough, North Yorkshire.**

ABOVE **Jellied eel bar at Hastings, East Sussex.**

ABOVE **Breakfast at the Harbour Lodge Guest House, Looe, Cornwall.**

ABOVE **Breakfast at Culver Lodge Hotel, Sandown, Isle of Wight.**

ABOVE Sweet Temptation at Hunstanton, Norfolk.

LEFT A tempting array of cakes on display in the window of Bothams Bakers, Whitby, North Yorkshire.

ABOVE Breakfast at the Anchorage Hotel, Whitby, North Yorkshire.

ABOVE Breakfast at the Dalmary Guest House, Paignton, Devon.

Famous people

During the height of 'sculpturemania' in the early years of the 20th century, many statues were erected at the seaside. Queen Victoria seems to have been the favourite. Other contenders were local people but it seems a bit of a lottery whether they warranted a monument, a bust, a blue plaque or nothing at all. For instance, at Sandgate near Folkestone, there is a memorial to Lieutenant General Sir John Moore who was killed at Corunna in 1809, but not one to H G Wells who wrote *Mr Kipps* there. Those to whom statues have been erected include General Gordon at Gravesend, Sir Charles Palmer at Jarrow, William Harvey at Folkestone, Captain Lewis Tregonwell at Bournemouth, Snooks the dog at Aldeburgh and Dan Dare at Southport. Blue plaques abound: Benjamin Britten at Lowestoft, Ladies Nelson and Byron at Exmouth, and Peter Cushing at Whitstable. A list of the great and the good associated with the seaside would soon reach telephone directory length, but we mustn't forget Lowry at Berwick-upon-Tweed, Logie Baird at Hastings and John Betjeman at the little church of St Enodoc, Trebetherick, Cornwall.

LEFT
A Blue Plaque marks the birthplace of Charles Dickens (1812–70) at Landport, Portsmouth, Hampshire.

RIGHT
A bust of Charles Dickens at Bleak House Museum, Broadstairs, Kent. This was his seaside holiday home and the inspiration for his famous novel *Bleak House*.

RIGHT
A sign on a house in Broadstairs.

LEFT
The last resting place of Dante Gabriel Rossetti (1828–82) at Birchington, Kent.

RIGHT
The gravestone of John Betjeman (1906–84) at St Enodoc's, Trebetherick, Cornwall.

LEFT
The statue of Captain Robert Falcon Scott, 'Scott of the Antarctic' (1868–1912), at Portsmouth Naval Dockyard, Hampshire.

RIGHT
Statue of Dolly Peel (1783–1857) at South Shields, Tyne and Wear. Fishwife, smuggler and local heroine.

ABOVE Memorial to Captain Matthew Webb (1848–83) at Dover, Kent. In 1875, he became the first ever person to swim the English Channel, from Dover to Calais.

RIGHT Memorial to Charles Rolls (1877–1910) at Dover. In 1910, he was the first person to fly from Dover to France and back without stopping.

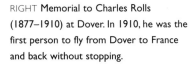

LEFT Memorial to Louis Bleriot (1872–1936) at Dover. In 1909, he was the first person to fly across the English Channel.

164

ABOVE Bust of Dame Agatha Christie (1890–1976), at Torquay, Devon. She was born in the town and spent much of her life in the area.

ABOVE Statue of Princess Pocahontas (1595–1617), at St George's Church, Gravesend, Kent, where she is reputedly buried.

BELOW Statue of Eric Morecambe (1926–84) in his familiar pose on the front at Morecambe, Lancashire. Sculpted by Graham Ibbeson, it was unveiled by the Queen in 1999.

ABOVE Statue of Captain James Cook (1728–79) at Whitby, North Yorkshire, the place where he began his seafaring career and from where he set off on many of his famous voyages.

Palmists and clairvoyants

Oracles, soothsayers, readers of the runes, seers, prophets, cheiromancers – all say they can reveal our destiny. Mind reading and fortune telling has always been popular at the seaside, but is it all a bit of fun with crystal balls and tea leaves, or is there some dark arcane truth behind it?

ABOVE **Madame Rene's** weatherboarded hut on the pier at Southend-on-Sea, Essex.

ABOVE **Lee Ester Alita Lee,** true born Romany clairvoyant and spiritualist at Whitby, North Yorkshire.

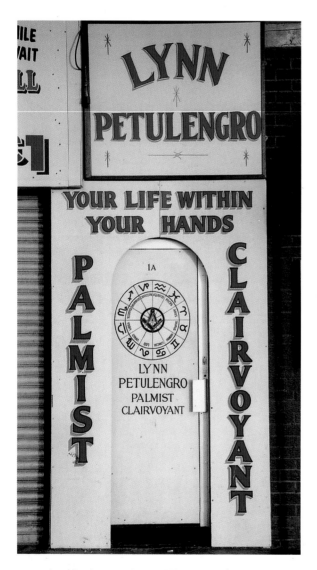

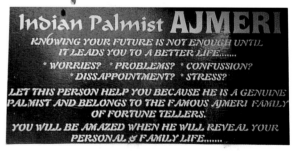

ABOVE **Lynn Petulengro,** palmist and clairvoyant at Skegness, Lincolnshire. The name Petulengro is thought to be of Egyptian origin and to mean blacksmith.

ABOVE **Ajmeri,** Indian palmist at Bridlington, East Yorkshire. Cheiro Ajmeri was taught the secrets of palmistry by the Brahmin Joshi caste of Vedic astrologers.

ABOVE Sign opposite the pier at Bognor Regis, West Sussex.

LEFT Gypsy Martha, palmist, clairvoyant and advice specialist at Bridlington, East Yorkshire.

BELOW Gypsy Margo, clairvoyant and palmist at Felixstowe, Suffolk.

ABOVE
A machine has taken over at Margate, Kent. The 'Lucky Lady' made by R S Coin outside the Royal Amusement Arcade.

Joke shops

Rather rare these days. Many joke shops have changed into 'fancy dress' shops. 'Whoopee cushions' and the like can now be bought on-line. Enjoy these while you can.

RIGHT **Art of the signwriter at the Joke Shop, Margate, Kent.**

ABOVE Jokes, magic, fancy dress and saucy items at The Joke Shop, Vaughan Parade, Torquay, Devon.

ABOVE **The Joke Shop in the Arlington Tower precinct at Margate, Kent.**

ABOVE **Old faithfuls** – the squirting lighter, itching powder and frothing blood.

ABOVE **Inflatable (and real!) cats at Minehead, Somerset.**

ABOVE **Giggles galore** at The Joke Shop, Scarborough, North Yorkshire. Not only hats, wigs and masks, but also magic and 'near miracles' are on offer.

RIGHT
The Harbourside Party Shop, Scarborough, North Yorkshire.

A nice cup of tea

There's a lot of walking up and down the prom. We have seen the sights and the tearoom is conveniently placed just where you can see there's no point in walking any further. It's only sensible to stop for a cuppa.

ABOVE A teapot sign hangs in the window of the Manor Tea Rooms, Sand Bay, Kewstoke, Somerset.

ABOVE Chalkboard sign at the Café Latino, Herne Bay, Kent.

RIGHT The Zambezi Tea Room at Bembridge, Isle of Wight.

BELOW Sea View Café at Tankerton, Kent.

LEFT Hellikers Tea Rooms, Watchet, Somerset. A 'proper' tea room.

BELOW 'Storm in a teacup' – one of the illuminations at Blackpool, Lancashire.

ABOVE Tea for two at the Tudor Tea Rooms, Whitstable, Kent. Favourite café of the late Peter Cushing.

RIGHT Tudor Tea Rooms sign at Whitstable, Kent.

Staring out to sea

Most people don't notice the
buildings – they sit facing the sea.
The principal reason for going to
the seaside, the edge of the land
(really the edge of the world), is
to see the horizon and to see
the future.

RIGHT **Sea-gazing at Folkestone, Kent.**

OPPOSITE PAGE **Near the Tyneside coast,
Tyne and Wear.**

BELOW **Bexhill-on-Sea, East Sussex.**

Acknowledgements

Thanks must go to the many people who have helped me during ten years of snapping away at the seaside. Thanks to Mike Hesketh-Roberts and James O. Davies; to Anne Williams who was a constant help and to Lisa Williams who accompanied me to the Kent coast; to Allan Brodie, Andrew Sargent, Gary Winter and particularly Ursula Dugard-Craig for advice, help and inspiration. Thanks also to Rob Richardson and Val Horsler for encouragement, to Sue Kelleher who helped me select the pictures, persuaded me to omit dodgy material and edited the text; to Shaun Watts who printed many of the photographs and Ian Leonard who worked on the cover, and to Rod Teasdale who has designed the book.

Index of places illustrated

A

Ainsdale, Merseyside 153
Aldeburgh, Suffolk 118
Amble by the Sea,
    Northumberland 55

B

Bamburgh, Northumberland 9, 31, 35
Barton-upon-Humber,
    Lincolnshire 49
Beachy Head, East Sussex 19
Bembridge, Isle of Wight 33, 91, 108,
    127, 170
Berrow, Somerset 26
Berwick-upon-Tweed,
    Northumberland 106
Bexhill-on-Sea, East Sussex 99, 172
Bill of Portland, Dorset 9
Birchington, Kent 150, 151, 156, 163
Blackpool, Lancashire 6, 70, 90, 91,100,
    104, 108, 119, 137, 138, 139, 146,
    151, 155, 159, 171
Bognor Regis, West Sussex 1, 167
Boscastle, Cornwall 50, 89
Boston, Lincolnshire 26
Bournemouth, Dorset 72, 88, 111, 116,
    120, 147
Bridlington, East Yorkshire 24, 78, 80,
    107, 112, 114, 149, 166, 167
Bridport, Dorset 97
Brightlingsea, Essex 14, 37, 79
Brighton, East Sussex 6, 54, 67, 73, 86,
    87, 110, 130, 139, 145, 147
Broadstairs, Kent 60, 154, 162
Budleigh Salterton, Devon 21, 108
Burnham on Crouch,
    Essex 40, 98
Burnham-on-Sea, Somerset 19

C

Caister-on-Sea, Norfolk 9, 33
California, Norfolk 154
Camber, East Sussex 27
Canvey Island, Essex 99, 158
Clacton-on-Sea, Essex 68, 140
Cleethorpes, Lincolnshire 65, 72, 123,
    134, 151
Clevedon, Somerset 74–5
Cowes, Isle of Wight 82
Craster, Northumberland 12
Cromer, Norfolk 24, 32, 53, 69, 71, 102,
    104
Cullercoats, Tyne and Wear 30

D

Dartmouth, Devon 45
Dawlish, Devon 123
Deal, Kent 22, 35
Dover, Kent 16, 34, 43, 106, 120, 164
Dungeness, Kent 19, 93, 95, 97, 126
Dymchurch, Kent 137

E

East Tilbury, Essex 38
Eastbourne, East Sussex 41, 52, 67, 68,
    71, 73, 76, 130, 157
Exmouth, Devon 23, 44

F

Falmouth, Cornwall 125, 131
Felixstowe, Suffolk 14, 82, 83, 117, 133,
    167
Filey, North Yorkshire 8, 12, 55, 83, 123,
    130, 149
Flamborough, East Yorkshire 11, 31
Fleetwood, Lancashire 15, 81, 141

Folkestone, Kent 57, 87, 136, 142, 146,
    172
Fowey, Cornwall 104
Frinton-on-Sea, Essex 101

G

Gorleston-on-Sea, Norfolk 16
Gravesend, Kent 165
Great Yarmouth, Norfolk 42, 123, 133,
    134

H

Happisburgh, Suffolk 18, 39
Hastings, East Sussex 12, 25, 85, 94, 98,
    160
Herne Bay, Kent 60, 62, 63, 100, 121,
    157, 170
Holy Island, Northumberland 27, 48
Hornsea, East Yorkshire 57, 82, 113
Hull, East Yorkshire 109
Hunstanton, Norfolk 112, 114, 144, 161
Hurst Spit, Hampshire 95
Hythe, Kent 36

I

Ilfracombe, Devon 15

K

Kewstoke, Somerset 16, 96, 170

L

Lamorna Cove, Cornwall 46
Leysdown-on-Sea, Kent 97
Lindisfarne, Northumberland 48, 125
Lizard, The, Cornwall 23
Looe, Cornwall 160
Lowestoft, Suffolk 32, 51, 97, 107
Lyme Regis, Dorset 20, 56, 61, 111

M

Mablethorpe, Lincolnshire 82, 141

Margate, Kent 51, 52, 53, 54, 64, 65, 73, 105, 107, 116, 133, 135, 143, 158, 167, 168

Minehead, Somerset 143, 150, 152, 168

Minster, Kent 47

Morecambe, Lancashire 101, 165

Mundesley, Norfolk 103

N

New Brighton, Merseyside 35, 87, 105

Newhaven, East Sussex 17, 105

Newlyn, Cornwall 11, 26

Newquay, Cornwall 11, 57, 88

North Shields, Tyne and Wear 15

P

Padstow, Cornwall 14

Paignton, Devon 69, 87, 88, 109, 116, 161

Pegwell Bay, Kent 46

Penzance, Cornwall 55

Pevensey, East Sussex 101

Plymouth, Devon 18, 42, 43, 54, 102

Polperro, Cornwall 10, 102

Poole, Dorset 118

Port Isaac, Cornwall 11

Porth Nanven, Cornwall 8

Portland Bill, Dorset 9, 19

Porthleven, Cornwall 38

Portsmouth, Hampshire 36, 37, 44, 45, 70, 162, 163

Potter Heigham, Norfolk 144

R

Ramsgate, Kent 50, 64, 109, 124, 128, 135, 157

Reculver, Kent 49

Redcar, North Yorkshire 29, 96, 120

Robin Hood's Bay, North Yorkshire 15

Roker, Tyne and Wear 47, 120

S

St Annes, Lancashire 32, 67, 102

St Ives, Cornwall 6, 29, 118, 121, 124

Saltburn-by-the-Sea, North Yorkshire 85, 103

Sandown, Isle of Wight 72, 77, 80, 111, 135, 152, 160

Sandwich, Kent 148

Scarborough, North Yorkshire 21, 35, 41, 56, 57, 65, 81, 84, 87, 103, 104, 105, 109, 113, 136, 140, 141, 155, 156, 159, 169

Seahouses, Northumberland 15, 19

Seaford, East Sussex 80

Shanklin, Isle of Wight 85, 89

Sheerness, Kent 20, 36, 40, 44

Sidmouth, Devon 104, 127

Silloth on Solway, Cumbria 158

Shellness, Kent 39, 92, 93

Shoreham by Sea, West Sussex 92, 93

Skegness, Lincolnshire 23, 56, 64, 70, 88, 113, 122, 125, 129, 134, 136, 137, 149, 153, 166

Snape, Suffolk 118

South Shields, Tyne and Wear 17, 28, 30, 116, 119, 163

Southampton 17

Southend-on-Sea, Essex 105, 128, 132, 144, 149, 154, 166

Southport, Merseyside 31, 53, 101, 107, 117, 122, 136, 138, 143, 146

Southsea, Hampshire 36, 43, 103, 105, 153

Southwold, Suffolk 12, 14, 21, 33, 77, 78, 79, 141

Staithes, Yorkshire 25

Spittal, Northumberland 106

Sunderland 120

Sutton Bridge, Lincolnshire 17

Sutton on Sea, Lincolnshire 94

Swanage, Dorset 38, 63

T

Tankerton, Kent 170

Tilbury, Essex 34

Tollesbury, Essex 95

Torquay, Devon 41, 66, 112, 165, 168

Trebetherick, Cornwall 163

Trusthorpe, Lincolnshire 104

Tynemouth, Tyne and Wear 30, 38, 55, 122, 158

Tyneside, Tyne and Wear 173

V

Ventnor, Isle of Wight 20, 22, 112

W

Walmer, Kent 127

Walton on the Naze, Essex 71, 79

Warden Point, Kent 40

Watchet, Somerset 45, 171

West Bay, Dorset 97

West Mersea, Essex 14

Weston super Mare, Somerset 68

Weymouth, Dorset 2, 22, 57, 58–9, 107, 117, 149

Whitby, North Yorkshire 15, 47, 54, 80, 115, 161, 165, 166

Whitby Scaur, North Yorkshire 27

Whitley Bay, Tyne and Wear 18, 23, 55, 103, 114, 122, 133, 151, 156

Whitstable, Kent 78, 95, 171

Winchelsea, East Sussex 96

Withernsea, East Yorkshire 49, 68, 113, 131

Workington, Cumbria 18

Worthing, West Sussex 13, 14, 67, 100, 154

Y

Yarmouth, Isle of Wight 29